DELETED IN THE DISTRICT

RAMBLING RV COZY MYSTERIES, BOOK 10

PATTI BENNING

SUMMER PRESCOTT BOOKS PUBLISHING

Copyright 2023 Summer Prescott Books

All Rights Reserved. No part of this publication nor any of the information herein may be quoted from, nor reproduced, in any form, including but not limited to: printing, scanning, photocopying, or any other printed, digital, or audio formats, without prior express written consent of the copyright holder.

**This book is a work of fiction. Any similarities to persons, living or dead, places of business, or situations past or present, is completely unintentional.

CHAPTER ONE

Going on a road trip around the country without visiting the nation's capital would have been a travesty, if you asked one Tulia Blake. Back in eighth grade, her class had gone on a field trip to the capital, but Tulia and a few other students had been out with the flu, and she had always regretted her lost chance at seeing such a historical city. There was no way she was missing out on it a second time. Even though she was itching to get up to Boston and visit Samuel, this was one stop she needed to make.

She had only just arrived at her hotel, and already, she wasn't disappointed. She had found a nice hotel with views of the Washington Monument on a tree-lined street within walking distance of the National

Mall, and she had liked the look of the suites enough that she had called to ask if their no-pets policy extended to birds.

Maybe it was because she wanted to book a suite for an entire week or maybe it was because birds tended to slip under the radar when it came to pet policies, but the hotel was happy to make an exception for her. And just like that, she and Cicero, her African Grey parrot, had a cozy place to stay right in the heart of the city. The lobby was modern and sleek, with a lot of glass and cream and black furniture. There was a whole wall dedicated to information about the area and opportunities for tourism. She made a mental note to come back and check it out later. Right now, she wanted to get checked in. She had already parked and put her luggage and Cicero's cage onto a trolley, so all that was left was getting her keycard and finding her way to her suite.

Other than a few curious glances at Cicero, check-in went smoothly. She got her keycard and followed the desk worker's directions down the hall to the elevator, which took her up to the fifth floor. Her suite was down the hallway to the left, past a series of quiet rooms with closed doors. This hotel felt like it was intended more for business than vacationing, unlike the resort in Florida, but the location couldn't be beat.

She found her suite easily and let herself in with the keycard. The modern decor continued into the suite itself, with a glass coffee table, a sleek, dark-blue couch, and a kitchen and bathroom both done in pristine white tile. The sitting room was open to the kitchen, but the bedroom was past a set of heavy, white sliding doors. She set Cicero's cage on the desk in the corner of the sitting room—she didn't want to risk scratching the lovely glass coffee table with it—and unloaded her luggage in the bedroom before pushing the trolley out into the hall. The person at the front desk had told her another staff member would come along to collect it shortly.

"Well, this is our home for the next week," she told Cicero.

The bird was clinging to the bars of his cage, looking around in blatant curiosity. They had been in quite a few different hotels during their trip, and each one had a different feel. She didn't think this hotel was her favorite by any means—she had really liked the more old-fashioned, Victorian-esque suite she'd had back in Louisiana—but it would certainly make for a comfortable week. She had parked her RV at a long-term parking lot outside of the city and had taken her sedan from there. She had been camping for the past week, so this would be a nice change of pace.

"You stay right there," she told Cicero. "I'll get you out of your cage in a few minutes. I want to unpack a little first."

She was never sure just how much her parrot understood, but she talked to him a lot just in case. He was smart, and besides, he could talk back.

After she tested the comfortable king-sized bed and unpacked her clothes into the chest of drawers, she took out her cell phone and sent off a pair of quick text messages, first to Samuel and then to her parents. Both messages had the same content.

Made it to my hotel. I'll send pictures soon and will call this evening!

She knew Samuel was in a meeting with a client, so he likely wouldn't respond, but her father texted back almost immediately.

Good! I was getting worried. What is your room number, sweetie?

She raised an eyebrow, wondering why on earth her father wanted to know that, but figured he was probably just being extra cautious after she got stranded at a campground without any service just over a week ago. He probably wanted to know how to track her down if it happened again.

520, she texted back. *It's a nice suite. Haven't*

explored it much yet. I'm probably going to stay in tonight and go do tourist stuff tomorrow. Don't worry, I'll send lots of pictures.

Her father sent a thumbs up. She rolled her eyes, waited a second to see if her mother would respond, and when she didn't, she stood up and took her laptop out of its bag. She carried it into the sitting room and opened Cicero's cage so he could climb on top of it, then sat down on the couch and propped the laptop open. She wouldn't start writing her blog post until later, but she'd gotten a few comments she wanted to respond to before she forgot. She glanced at her phone again while she waited for the computer to connect to the hotel's Internet and frowned. Her mother hadn't responded to any text messages since earlier that morning. She would be worried, but it was a weekend, and she knew both of her parents were at home and her father would certainly have told her if something was wrong. Her mother must just be busy —sometimes she embarked on cleaning or baking projects that took all day. She would get a chance to talk to her when she called later tonight.

After checking her travel blog and replying to a few of the comments on her last post, she shut her laptop, put Cicero back into his cage, made sure she had her wallet, her keycard, and her phone, then left the hotel room. The trolley in front of her door was gone, but two more had taken its place just down the hall, near the elevator. These were still half-full of luggage and were half blocking the hall. She stepped around the first trolley and almost ran smack-dab into a younger woman with pale highlights in her auburn hair.

"Excuse me," the woman snapped.

"Sorry," Tulia replied, a little shocked at the aggression in the woman's voice.

"Robin, did you really have to bring so much?" a man who looked to be about the woman's age said as he came out of the room and heaved another heavy suitcase off of the trolley. It was bright pink and seemed to be part of a matched set.

"I want to look my best while we're visiting your parents, you know that," the woman replied in the exact same tone of voice she had used to snap at Tulia. "I've seen how your mother travels, and she is just as bad as I am, if not worse."

Tulia edged past them and continued down the hall past the second trolley, which was between two of the neighboring rooms. Two men were unloading the trolley and carrying their luggage into their separate rooms. One looked to be in his fifties and the other around Tulia's age, in his thirties. The younger of the two looked at the arguing couple and rolled his eyes. The older just shook his head, looking annoyed. When he saw Tulia, he nodded, then grabbed his suitcase.

Tulia was glad to leave the squabbling couple behind as she got into the elevator. While she wouldn't have turned Samuel down if he offered to travel with her for a while, there were certain benefits to traveling alone.

She had no one to carry her luggage, true, but she also didn't have to share an itinerary with anyone or change her plans to accommodate anyone else's needs. She could do whatever struck her fancy, which was a freedom she was enjoying quite a bit, especially after wasting two years of her life with Luis.

In the lobby, she meandered over to the display of information about the local attractions, of which there were quite a few. She wanted to visit the National Mall and the Washington Monument, of course, and she wanted to at least see the White House from the outside. But she also wanted to see the rest of the city and visit a few museums. There was no way she was going to come all this way and not see the Smithsonian.

She gathered her pamphlets and, armed with

information, headed back to the elevator and up to her floor. The two empty trolleys were sitting next to their respective rooms, and as she walked past the one with the young couple inside, she could hear their squabbling, even through the closed door, though she couldn't make out the individual words. Thankfully, her suite was far enough down the hall that she couldn't hear them once she got to it, and when she shut her door behind her, she was greeted by complete silence. Well, after a whistle of greeting from Cicero.

She let him out of his cage again and took a few pictures of her suite, then settled down on the couch to look through the pamphlets and start a new blog post. Writing her blog posts always relaxed her, and the time flew by as she typed, formatted, and added some of the photos to her post.

She had arrived at the hotel in the early hours of the evening, and it was beginning to get dark out by the time she finished her post. She had ended the post with a question to her readers, asking for recommendations of things to do and see in the city, but she had already decided to see the Smithsonian first. She'd go in the morning tomorrow, then find somewhere fun to eat for lunch.

"We made it, buddy," she told Cicero, getting up

to refill his food bowl. "We're in the nation's capital. We've only got another month or so before we return home."

It was a bittersweet thought. She hadn't seen all of the states yet, but she did want to touch base back at home and get started on figuring out what she was going to do with the rest of her life before she set out again. She had driven around the perimeter of the country, but she still had to see most of the interior states, as well as Alaska and Hawaii. And who said her travels had to end there? She could afford a flight across the ocean now. The only thing holding her back from seeing other countries was how intimidated she felt by the thought of traveling to a foreign place alone.

She gave Cicero some fresh water and food and was on her way back to the couch when someone knocked at her suite's door. She frowned. She hadn't ordered room service, and she didn't think they would send anyone in to clean until tomorrow at the earliest. She forced the instinctive surge of fear down and reminded herself that Luis was behind bars. He couldn't follow her any longer.

She moved over to the door and looked out the peephole, then took a step back, rubbed her eyes, and looked out the peephole again, not sure if what she was seeing was real. Finally, feeling utterly confused and wondering if this was some sort of strange dream, she unlocked the door and pulled it open.

"Mom?"

CHAPTER TWO

"Tulia! I've missed you so much. Oh, come here. I need to hug you."

Tulia's mother, Melissa Blake, rushed forward and enveloped her in a hug. Tulia was stiff as a board until, slowly, the familiar feel of her mother's arms around her thawed her enough to return the hug.

"I don't understand. What are you doing here?"

Her mother pulled back, beaming at her. "It's a surprise visit. Your father and I were talking last week about how much we missed you, and I knew you were coming up here to Washington, so just for fun I checked for flights, and there was a really cheap round trip available. I bought it up as soon as I saw it. Your father couldn't get off work for the week, but

I'm here. It's been so long since I've seen you, sweetie. You look different."

Her mother took another step back, looking her up and down from head to toe. Tulia shifted, still fuzzy with shock.

"You just bought a plane ticket and flew out here to visit me out of the blue? Why didn't you say anything?"

Her mother's face fell. "I wanted it to be a surprise. Are you upset?"

"No, no," Tulia said quickly. "Of course not, I'm just surprised, that's all. I wasn't expecting to see you. Come on in."

She stepped back. Her mother came in and shut the door, then made a beeline over to Cicero's cage. The parrot had grown up with her parents as much as she had, and he was excited to see her.

Tulia just stood there, watching as her mother gently scratched the soft feathers on the bird's head. Her mother was … here. In Washington DC, with her.

"How long can you stay?" she asked after a second.

"All the way until Friday," her mother said cheerfully. "Now, I can get a room at another hotel if you don't have room for me here. I think there are some cheap ones on the other side of town. I took a cab from the airport, but maybe I can find a rental car—"

"No, no, you're welcome to stay here," Tulia said. She blinked, shook herself, and tried to get her mind back in gear. It *was* nice to see her mother, she just had to readjust her expectations for the week. "The couch pulls out into a bed. You can take the master bedroom if you want."

"Nonsense, I'm not going to take your bed from you after springing all of this on you. I'm happy with the pullout. And how are *you* doing, my handsome boy?" she crooned, leaning down to kiss Cicero on his beak.

Tulia smiled, beginning to feel like she had her feet under her again. Her mother was visiting for the week. Surprising, yes. Unpleasant? Definitely not. She really *had* missed her parents, and it would be fun to explore the city with her mother.

"So, what plans did you have for this evening?" her mother asked. "Have you eaten yet? All I had on the plane were a few of those cookies they give you midflight. If you're not hungry, I'll probably just order a cheap pizza for myself."

"I haven't eaten," Tulia admitted, moving back over toward the couch. She flopped down on it, still trying to wrap her mind around just how much her week had changed. "Do you want to get room service? I'm sure this place has decent food."

"Room service is usually expensive, isn't it?" her mother said hesitantly. Tulia felt her heart clench. Her parents weren't poor, but they were firmly middle class, and her mother wasn't the type to spend money when she didn't have to. Random plane tickets excluded, apparently.

"Mom, did you forget I won the lottery?" she asked, raising an eyebrow. "I am more than happy to pay for all of our food during this trip. Trust me when I say I won't even notice that the money's gone. Treat yourself. I'm serious. We can eat wherever you want, do whatever you want, and I'll take care of all of it." She had already offered to pay off her parents' mortgage, but they had refused. She was determined to do this for her mother at the very least, so she held the older woman's gaze as she hesitated.

"Oh, sweetie, I just wouldn't feel right—"

"Mom, I'm serious," Tulia said, her voice firm. "Don't be weird about this, please. Everyone gets weird around me when they learn I won the lottery. I can't handle that from you and Dad too. Just let me buy our food and pay for our activities. I really want to do something nice for you."

"Well, all right," her mother said, biting her lip.

"If you're sure." Her face relaxed into a smile. "Thank you, Tulia. I appreciate it, I really do. I just don't want you to think your father and I would ever take advantage of you."

"I know you wouldn't," Tulia assured her. "But you have to see how silly it is to insist on buying everything yourself when your wonderful daughter won the lottery half a year ago. It's just common sense. Now, where did that room service menu go? What are you in the mood for?" Her stomach rumbled. "I think I'm leaning toward some pasta, myself."

They looked over the menu and called in their order. While they waited, they sat on the couch, and Tulia and her mother looked through the pamphlets she had brought up from the lobby.

"There's so much to do," her mother said. "What did you want to do first?" Tulia opened her mouth to mention the Smithsonian, but her mother had focused on another one of the pamphlets. "Oh, look at this. It's a tour of the city, and they hit all of the most popular sites. And they have a tour leaving tomorrow morning. This might be a good place to start, because the places we like the most, we can visit later in the week. It will give us an idea of what we want to see."

Tulia shut her mouth. That was ... actually a pretty good idea.

"Sure. We should sign up tonight, so they don't fill up," Tulia said. "If they're open, that is. I'll call them and see if they can fit us in."

She dialed the number on the pamphlet and was half expecting it to go to voicemail, but someone answered. She mentioned her interest in the tour leaving at ten o'clock on Monday morning, and the woman on the other end said, "Oh, you're just in time. We had another group sign up for that same tour just a few minutes ago. How many are your party?"

"Just two of us," Tulia said.

"Perfect. We can fit you in. I'll need your names and your credit card information. The tour bus will leave from your hotel at ten o'clock sharp. We ask you to be in the lobby to meet with your group no later than nine fifty-five. Unfortunately, we can't delay the bus if you're late. The tour lasts an average of five hours, but that's dependent on traffic and wait times. You'll stop at a cafe for lunch at noon but will have to pay for your own food. We suggest everyone brings a water bottle, some cash, and of course, a camera."

Tulia gave the woman her card information, thanked her, and ended the call.

"We're all set," she told her mother. "We leave tomorrow at ten."

Her mother reached across the couch to squeeze her hand. "I'm so excited," she said. "It's so nice to see you again, sweetie. This is going to be an amazing week."

Tulia smiled and squeezed her mother's hand back. "Yeah, it really is."

CHAPTER THREE

Tulia and her mother stayed up late enjoying their meal and watching an old, black and white movie on the television. Before going to bed, Tulia made another attempt at convincing her mother to take the master bedroom, but her mother declined, insistent upon sleeping on the pullout couch.

She set her alarm for eight the next morning and woke up to sunshine streaming through the curtains. Careful to keep quiet in case her mother was still sleeping, she went into the bathroom for a shower. Once she was done, she stepped into the living area to see that her mother had already made them both cups of coffee. Cicero was on top of his cage, and her mother had chopped up a banana for him for breakfast. The bird seemed happy to have another family member around.

"I'm going to go get ready," her mother said. "Then let's head down to breakfast."

Tulia had gotten used to living by her own beat while she was on the road. Maybe too used to it. It was a little strange to have someone else hurrying her along and commenting on all of the food options at the breakfast buffet. Tulia kept her food light, wanting to treat herself for lunch without worrying about the calories, but even so, breakfast took longer than usual because her mother kept pausing between bites to chat. The two of them took a picture together to send to her father, and Tulia sent it to Samuel as well. She'd updated him about her mother's visit the night before, and now she told him all about their plans for the day.

They were in the lobby and ready to go by nine fifty. Tulia had been a little concerned about finding the right group to leave with, but there was a man holding a sign with the tour company's name on it standing near the front doors. There were already four other people there, and Tulia recognized them as the other guests from her floor, whom she'd run into the day before. They were all dressed to the nines, and the woman, Robin, gave Tulia and her mother a disdainful look as they joined the group.

"… three … four … five … six," the man holding the sign said. "We've got the Danons and the Blakes, right?" They nodded. "That's everyone, then. A small group today. If any of you need to run to the restroom or grab a bottle of water, now is the time. We will be breaking for lunch in two hours. After lunch, we will be going to a lovely park to stretch our legs. Is everyone ready? Good. Follow me outside, where our bus is waiting." He paused. "Oh, I'm Dan Berger, your tour guide for today. You can call me Dan, Mr. Berger, or Hey, you!" He chuckled. "Any or all of those work. Your bus driver is Julian McKinney. He's been with the company for twenty years, and he knows DC like the back of his hand, so you can rely on him to get us around safely."

They followed him outside to see a small dark-blue bus with the company's logo on the side. Tulia followed her mother up the steps and was glad to find that it looked clean and comfortable. Dan was the last one on the bus and stood at the head of the aisle while they found their seats. Tulia and her mother sat at the front, and the young couple sat across the aisle from them. The other two men sat separately, the one in his thirties behind the young couple and the older man behind Tulia and her mother. Before Dan could say anything, Robin glanced over at Tulia and her mother and said, "I thought we were the only ones who were signed up for this tour, RJ."

RJ patted her hand. "The woman on the phone said we were the only ones to sign up so far. They must've signed up after we did. It's not a problem, Robin. You've never seen DC before. Just relax and enjoy yourself."

Behind Tulia, the older man chuckled. "Robin relaxing and enjoying herself? That'll be the day."

Next to Robin, RJ turned in his seat and shot the man a glare. "If you're just going to be rude to my fiancée, you don't have to come, Uncle Victor."

The man in the seat behind RJ and Robin sighed. He looked similar enough to RJ that Tulia thought they were probably related. "Can all of you please just cool it? This is supposed to be a celebration. Can't we all just get along and have a good time?"

"This family, getting along and having a good time?" Victor chuckled. "That'll be the day. I didn't think you were so naïve, Alex."

"I should be able to spend one day with my uncle, my brother, and his fiancée without fighting," Alex snapped back. "Besides, we're here to celebrate my promotion. If you don't want to be polite for a few days, you can leave." He cleared his throat, faced forward, and fixed his eyes on Dan.

"I'm so sorry for the interruption. Please, just ignore my family. They'll settle down once the tour gets started."

Dan gave a strained smile. "Of course. Everyone, please buckle up. Welcome to Washington DC. What brings you here?"

He looked at Tulia first, so she replied, "I'm taking a road trip around the country, and my mom is here to visit me."

"We're here celebrating me nephew's promotion at his father's company," Victor said, nodding over at Alex.

"Both things sound wonderful," Dan said. "I hope you enjoy this tour. First, we will be driving past the National Mall and the Washington Monument. I'm sure all of you saw the Washington Monument on your approach to the hotel." They all buckled in, and the bus jolted into motion. Dan held onto a handhold and continued talking. "You may be interested to know that it took over forty years to complete construction on the Washington Monument. Construction began in 1848 but was later halted due to a lack of funds. It wasn't finished until 1888. It was the tallest structure in the world until the Eiffel Tower was built in Paris…"

Tulia settled back into her seat and looked out the window as Dan continued speaking. Going on a tour today might not have been her first choice, but she was glad her mother had thought of it.

The tour took them past the White House that morning and ended at a small café near a park. As the six of them filed out of the bus, Dan hung back and chatted with the driver.

"Julian is going to go refuel. He'll pick us up in half an hour, so we have time to eat and stretch our legs for a while. Restrooms are just around the corner. This place has delicious sandwiches and some very good cappuccinos if you need a pick-me-up."

Tulia got a turkey Havarti sandwich on toasted brioche bread for herself, while her mother opted for a chicken salad sandwich. They waited while the others ordered, then picked up their food and walked over to the park. It was a nice day, and no one complained about sitting at a picnic table with their food. Though the other four people in their group kept to themselves, Tulia and her mother sat at the other end of the table with Dan.

"This must be such an interesting job," Tulia's mother said as they unwrapped their food. "Why did you choose to be a tour guide?"

Dan smiled. "Well, I've lived here my whole life, and I got tired of working an office job. This way, I get to ride around in a bus all day, talk to a lot of interesting people, and I leave with tips in my pocket every evening." He winked. "The company I work for partners with local hotels, and the work is pretty steady. Plus, I love my city. Have either of you been to DC before?"

Tulia shook her head. "No, but I've always wanted to come here. I knew I couldn't miss it when I had the chance."

"Where are you from?"

"Michigan," Tulia's mother said. "But Tulia here has been all over the US by now. She's taking a road trip around the country."

"Oh," Dan said, his eyes lighting up. "That must be a lot of fun. I've always wanted to do something like that. Maybe when I retire."

They continued chatting while they finished their sandwiches, then dispersed to walk around for a little while. Dan advised them to all meet back at the bus stop at the edge of the park at twelve thirty. Tulia and her mother spent some time watching a few ducks play in a pond before wandering back toward the bus stop, where the other members of their group were already waiting. They were talking amongst themselves, or rather, arguing.

"I know we're not supposed to go back to the hotel until three, but I want to get back sooner," Robin was saying. "I just got a notification that the nail salon I want to go to has an opening, and I want to get my nails done before your parents come this evening."

"Well, maybe Dan will make an exception," RJ said. He turned to the tour guide. "Would you be willing to drop my fiancée off at the hotel? I know it's out of your way, but we would really appreciate it."

"I'm sorry, but the company doesn't allow me to make changes to our route for anything other than major traffic incidents."

"I'll make it worth your while," RJ said, fishing for his wallet. "Could you do it for a fifty?"

"It's policy. I can't," Dan said. "Julian will be back soon. Let's move down a little further. We need to leave room for the city bus if it comes." He led them a little way down from the bus stop, and they gathered together by the curb.

"Look, surely it won't be too much of a delay if you—" RJ started.

His brother, Alex, cut in. "Just drop it, man," he

said. "I'll buy a cab for Robin if she wants to get back so badly. Does that work?"

Robin wrinkled her nose. "I really don't like taking cabs. I don't like riding with strangers."

Alex sighed and ran his hand through his hair. Victor laughed, seeming amused by all of this, and lit a cigarette to smoke while they waited. "And I thought your mother was spoiled. You've really outdone yourself with this one, RJ."

"Leave her be," RJ growled.

"I'm not spoiled," Robin snapped. "I just don't want to get into a dirty cab with a stranger."

"This is ridiculous," Alex said. He turned to Dan. "Look, I'll pay you a hundred bucks just to take us back to the hotel early. I can't stand listening to her whine and moan for the rest of the trip."

"Hey!" Robin said, offended.

"Alex—" RJ started at the same time Dan spoke.

"It's policy—"

"I don't care what your policy is," Alex cut in. "Two hundred. Cash. That's got to be more than you'd make all day otherwise."

Dan ground his teeth together, beginning to get angry. Tulia edged away from the group, wanting to avoid the argument. Her mother tugged on her sleeve, pointing into the park.

"Look, that woman has a macaw. We should bring Cicero here on his harness. I bet he'd like to see the ducks."

"Wow, that bird is a lot bigger than Cicero," Tulia said, watching the woman walking with the big blue and yellow macaw on her arm. "I don't know many other people with parrots. I wonder if I have time to go ask her if I can take a picture of her macaw?" Her blog readers would probably love to see it. The woman glanced up at them, and Tulia realized with some embarrassment she had seen her mother pointing.

"Well, why don't you ask—" her mother began, turning back toward the others just as a man shouted. Tulia spun around just in time to see Alex stumble backward off the curb. A horn sounded, and a city bus that was rushing toward the bus stop squealed its brakes, but it was too late.

The bus impacted Alex with a thud, throwing him across the pavement. His head hit the curb when he landed, and he lay frighteningly still in the chaos that followed.

CHAPTER FOUR

Robin screamed. RJ wrapped his arms around her and pulled her to his chest while Victor just stood there, his cigarette dangling from his fingers as he gaped at his nephew's still form. Dan was the only one of them who reacted, rushing forward to kneel next to Alex.

"Do something!" Robin shouted from where she was enclosed in RJ's arms. "He's bleeding!"

"He has a head injury," Dan said. "I'm not sure if I should touch him. Someone, please call an ambulance."

The bus driver got out, and Tulia could see him shaking as he hurried over to Alex and asked if he was all right. None of the others seemed to be taking their phones out, so she slipped her hand into her purse and pulled out her cell phone. Beside her, her mother had both her hands pressed to her lips.

Tulia dialed 911. She told the dispatcher what had happened but had to get Dan's attention to get their exact location.

"They're sending an ambulance," she told the others. "They say not to move him. Is he breathing?"

"I can't tell," Dan said. "I think so."

People were beginning to crowd around them. Victor finally broke from his stupor and stumbled forward, staring down at the man on the ground. "Alex?" he said. "Come on, buddy. It was just a tumble. You're all right, aren't you?"

Alex remained still and didn't move even after the ambulance arrived. The paramedics had them all step back as they began working on Alex. Using a neck brace and a stretcher, they got him loaded into the back of the ambulance. They told Alex's brother and uncle which hospital they were taking him to, then left in a flurry of flashing lights and sirens. The police were already there and had begun questioning people. Tulia and her mother hung back, watching while the police talked to Alex's family and then Dan and the bus driver. Finally, one of the officers approached them.

"Good afternoon, ladies," he said. "Did either of

you see what happened? There seems to be some confusion surrounding the incident."

"We weren't facing the right direction," Tulia said. "We were looking into the park. I didn't turn around until I heard him shout."

"I saw him out of the corner of my eye," her mother said. "It was horrible." She took a deep breath. "Someone pushed him."

Victor looked around at her words, his brow furrowing. Tulia looked at her mother too, surprised.

"Did you see who?" the officer asked, suddenly intently interested.

Tulia's mother shook her head. "I didn't. But he was just standing there, right next to the curb, and I saw his body jolt suddenly. He definitely didn't just trip and fall."

"Who else was standing near him?" the officer asked. "Could you show me where you were standing?"

They nodded and moved back to where they had been standing. "It was our entire tour group," Tulia's mother said. "My daughter and I, Alex's family, and Dan, our tour guide. Dan was talking to Alex and his family. Robin, the woman, wanted to go back to the hotel early. It all happened so fast."

The officer frowned. "Am I correct that the only

people who could have pushed him are the people in your tour group?"

Tulia's mother nodded. "It had to have been one of them."

"I see. We're going to be looking for a recording of the incident. Someone has to have a camera that caught it. Just in case we don't find anything and need to question you further, I'll need your name and some contact information. How long are you planning on being in town?"

Tulia and her mother gave him their information. Slowly, the crowd began to disperse. No one else, including Tulia, had seen Alex be pushed, and the bus driver himself hadn't seen a thing until the last moment. He admitted he had been looking down to change the radio station when he hit Alex. Tulia felt bad for him even though he hadn't been paying attention. If her mother was right and someone had pushed Alex, then the bus driver shouldn't be responsible for all of the blame.

Their bus had arrived at some point during all the commotion. After the police finished taking their statements and Tulia, her mother, and Alex's family were cleared to go for the time being, they all filed back into the bus. RJ and Robin took their old seats, and Victor sat behind them. The three of them were talking quietly as the bus started moving, heading back to the hotel. Dan didn't say anything either, just sat silently up front near the bus driver. It was a somber ride, and neither Tulia nor her mother spoke until Victor looked over at them and said, "Did you really see someone push him?"

Robin gasped. RJ wrapped an arm around her shoulders.

"She said someone pushed him?" he said. "That's ridiculous. We were the only people near him."

"That's why I'm asking her about it," Victor said. "I overheard her talking to the cops."

"I did see someone push him," Tulia's mother said. "I didn't see who, but I saw enough to know he definitely didn't just trip and fall."

"If you didn't see who pushed him, then how do you know someone did?" RJ asked, sounding irritated.

"Because I saw him jolt suddenly out of the corner of my eye. He only stepped off the curb after that. If he fell on his own, he would've stepped backward off the curb first, before falling. No one suddenly goes stumbling back from a standstill without an outside force acting on them."

RJ frowned but was distracted by Robin, who had started crying loudly into his chest. He comforted his fiancée. From the seat behind them, Victor sighed.

"Look, Alex has always been the sort to fool around. He was probably doing something dumb like trying to balance on the curb when he slipped and fell. I'm not saying you're lying, but you must be mistaken. Think about what you're saying. The only people who were close enough to push him were his family, or our tour guide."

"I don't understand how none of you saw anything," Tulia's mother said. "Like you said, you were all standing right there."

"We were looking in the direction you were pointing," RJ snapped. "We heard you tell your daughter about some big bird you saw. It's human reflex to look when someone else points. I don't think any of us were looking at Alex when he fell."

"What about the tour guide?" Robin asked, her voice warbling. "He was standing right next to Alex."

They all glanced toward Dan, who seemed to be studiously ignoring them. Tulia sighed. "Just let it go, Mom. The police have all the same information we have, and they'll sort it out."

"I know what I saw. *You* believe me, don't you?"

Tulia hesitated. She believed that her mom thought she had seen something, but it wasn't impossible that her mother was mistaken. It had all happened so fast. Her mother gave her a wounded look, but before either of them could say anything, Victor's phone started ringing.

He took it out of his pocket, frowned down at it, and said, "I don't recognize the number. It's a local area code."

"It could be the hospital," RJ said. "You should answer it. You gave the paramedics your phone number, didn't you?"

"I did. Your parents are still on their plane. If the hospital needed something, I wanted them to be able to get ahold of me." He hesitated, then hit the button to answer the call. Tulia couldn't hear what the person on the other line was saying, but she saw Victor's face go pale. He nodded, muttered something, and ended the call, then looked at RJ and Robin with wide eyes.

"He didn't make it," he whispered, his voice full of stunned shock. "He was declared dead when they reached the hospital."

CHAPTER FIVE

The instant the tour bus pulled up in front of the hotel, they clustered around the exit, eager to get out. Alex's brother and uncle had both sat in silence while Robin cried. No one else had dared say a thing in the face of their loss, but Tulia realized her mother's accusation about Alex being pushed had changed from an accusation of assault, to one of murder.

Everyone got off the bus besides Dan and the bus driver. Dan had been silent the entire ride, and as Tulia looked back at him while she descended the bus's steps, she saw him gazing off into the distance with a blank look in his eyes. She had no doubt that this was the worst tour he had ever given.

Wanting to give RJ, Robin, and Victor their privacy on the elevator ride back up to their rooms,

Tulia and her mother lingered in the lobby for a few minutes. Gazing out the windows, she watched as the bus pulled away. Hopefully, Dan wouldn't lose his job over this. Though, in retrospect, perhaps he shouldn't have had them waiting so close to the curb.

Once they were sure the Danons had enough time to take the elevator up to the fifth floor, Tulia and her mother called it back down and took it up by themselves. As they walked down the hall toward their suite, they could hear voices coming from the closed door of RJ and Robin's room. They didn't linger or try to eavesdrop; the family deserved their privacy, even if Tulia's mother had her doubts.

"What a horrible experience," her mother said as soon as they stepped into their suite. Tulia shut the door behind her, turning the deadbolt for a little bit of extra security. Cicero whistled a greeting from his cage. As soon as she got her shoes off, she went over to greet him, opening his cage and letting him climb out on his own.

"I know," Tulia said. "I feel horrible for everyone involved."

"Someone killed that man," her mother said. "I know what I saw."

"You didn't *see* anything, though, Mom. You

didn't actually see someone push him. You just saw him fall."

Her mother frowned. "I knew it. You don't believe me."

"I do," Tulia hedged. "Well, I believe that *you* believe what you're saying, but I think there's a possibility you were mistaken."

"Tulia, you tell me how a man can be standing perfectly still, only to suddenly jolt and stumble backward if no one pushed him."

"I'm just saying, it's a serious accusation. Maybe he … I don't know, had a stroke or something. Or maybe you're remembering wrong, and he did take a step back off the curb and overbalanced."

"I would believe *you* if you told me you saw something like that," her mother said. "I'm not wrong about this, Tulia. I saw what I saw."

"Then one of them killed him," Tulia said. "Either his brother, his brother's fiancée, his uncle, or the tour guide. That's what you're saying if you seriously believe he was pushed."

"You heard them arguing," her mother said, crossing her arms. "None of them seemed to particularly like each other. They wouldn't have had to mean for him to *die*. It could've just been a simple shove, something that was meant to get emotion across but not actually hurt him. A terrible mistake, not premeditated murder. You're an only child, Tulia, so you don't know what having siblings is like, but trust me when I say your aunt and I squabbled a *lot* when we were children."

"Yeah, when you were *children*," Tulia pointed out. "You don't go around shoving her into traffic now that you're both fully grown adults."

"Some people don't act their age even when they're adults." Her mother huffed. "I don't want to spend this trip arguing with you. Can we change the subject?"

"Yeah." Tulia sighed. "For the record, I'm not saying I think you're wrong. I just think we should keep an open mind. That's all."

"All right." Her mother approached Cicero's cage and scratched the bird on his head. "Well, what would you like to do for the rest of the day? We just had lunch, so getting food is out, and I doubt I would have much of an appetite anyway. If you don't have anything else in mind, I might go lie down for a little bit. I'm still shaken by what happened."

"You can go lie on my bed if you want," Tulia said. "I'm going to call Samuel, I think."

Her mother gave her a curious look Tulia knew all

too well. "The mysterious Samuel. When are you going to introduce him to your father and me?"

"When you guys aren't literally states away from each other," Tulia said, making shooing motions with her hands. "Go on, Mom. Privacy. It's a thing."

Her mother gave a good-natured sigh. Tulia watched as she walked into the bedroom and shut the sliding doors behind her, then pulled her phone out of her purse. She was still shaken by what had happened, but she was probably better prepared to handle something like this than her mother was. The sad truth was, she had seen far too much death over the past few months.

She picked Cicero up and carried him with her over to the glass coffee table, which she let him walk around on. He seemed fascinated by the transparent surface and kept pausing to knock his beak against it before peering down at the floor. She would just have to remember to sanitize it when she put him away, but at least there was no way his claws would damage the glass.

Once she was sure he was entertained rather than freaked out, she sent a quick text message to Samuel asking if he was available to talk. He called her a moment later.

"Hey."

"Hey," he said. "Is everything all right? I thought you and your mother had a guided tour this afternoon."

"Let's just say it didn't go as planned." She sighed. "One of the people we were with on the tour got hit by a bus. He didn't make it."

Samuel was silent for a second before saying, "How did that even happen? Tulia, you have the worst luck of anyone I've ever met. Are you and your mother okay?"

"We're shaken up, but we are fine overall. My mom thinks someone pushed him in front of the bus, but no one else saw anything. I don't know what to believe. I mean, obviously, neither myself nor my mother pushed him. The only other people around were some of his family members and our tour guide. I just can't see any of them doing it, but my mom is adamant that's what happened."

"Well, at least this sounds like it has nothing to do with you," he said. "Either of you. I'm sure the police have it all in hand. Still, if you want me to come down there, I will. I can talk to Marc about putting the case I'm working on off for a few days."

"No, no," she said. "You don't need to do that, Samuel. I just needed someone to talk to."

"Well, I can do that as well. What are your plans for the rest of the week?"

"I'd really like to see the Smithsonian sometime soon, and I want my mom to pick a few things to see and do as well. I'm going to feel weird about going out and having a good time today after what happened, though. I think we might just stay in until tomorrow."

Some vacation this is turning out to be, she thought as Samuel replied, offering a few suggestions of his own. Between the surprise visit from her mother and the possible murder, things had really gone off the rails.

CHAPTER SIX

They ordered room service that evening, and the next morning, they made sure Cicero was settled in his cage with some fresh fruit from the hotel's breakfast bar in his bowl, then headed out to the Smithsonian.

They toured the Natural History Museum first, and Tulia could barely take her eyes off the reconstructed remnants of prehistoric creatures. She had never considered herself a history buff, but seeing these creatures that walked the earth long before modern humans did filled her with awe. They had just enough time to see the American History Museum before their stomachs started growling and they had to call it off for lunch. Tulia wanted to see the rest of the complex later, but her mother was tired, so it would have to wait.

They stopped for sushi on their way back to the hotel. Treating her mom to a nice meal was fun, and Tulia began silently plotting how she could convince her parents to let her pay for the two of them to take a trip of their own. Even though they had squabbled a little the day before, Tulia was glad overall that her mother had come down for the surprise visit. It really was good to see her again.

"You must have so much fun out here on your own," her mother said as they ate. "Don't get me wrong, I love my life with your father, and I wouldn't trade it for the world, but I would have loved to have freedom like this when I was your age. You can go anywhere, do anything, eat out as many times a week as you want. I'm so happy for you, sweetie."

"Trust me, I know how lucky I am. I really hope I never take it for granted," Tulia said. "I'm really glad I took this trip, even with—" She broke off. Her parents knew a little about her more dangerous adventures, but not the full extent of them. Thankfully, her mother seemed to think she was referencing the bus accident from the day before and gave her a sad smile.

"Do you think you're going to settle down in Michigan when you come home?" Her mother sounded a little worried, and Tulia understood why.

She had just seen the world—well, more of it than she'd ever seen before. Would her very average hometown of Midland, Michigan, be enough to keep her in the state?

"I'm not sure," she admitted as she picked up a piece of her tempura shrimp roll with her chopsticks. "I haven't decided what I want to do long term yet. I know I want to use my money to make some sort of positive difference in the world, but that's about as far as I've gotten when it comes to my life plans. I *do* plan on spending some time at home before leaving again, though. I don't think I'll be done traveling yet, but I won't go running off right away. I miss you and Dad and my friends. Even if I do end up living somewhere other than Michigan, I'll still see you plenty, Mom. I can afford to fly back home once a month or fly you and Dad out to wherever I live. I love you, and I'm not going to just disappear."

"I know you won't, sweetie. And I don't want you to hold yourself back just for us. It doesn't mean I won't miss you, but at least I'll also be happy for you."

She might have bad luck when it came to dangerous encounters, but she had extremely good luck when it came to her family. She had never imagined that her life would take the turn it had, and she was beyond grateful that her parents had been as supportive and kind as they were.

When they got back to the hotel, they went to the lobby instead of straight up to their suite. Her mother wanted to look through some of the pamphlets that Tulia had skipped over to see if there was anything she wanted to do.

"Oh, we could go to the zoo," her mother said as she poured over the pamphlets. "It's free. You used to love going to the zoo, Tulia."

"Sure, that sounds like fun," Tulia said. Her attention was only half on the conversation. Her eyes were focused on the front desk. She had spotted Dan when they walked in and had assumed he was there to pick up another tour group, though in retrospect, it seemed odd that the company was running another tour the day after one of their clients died. It seemed her assumption was wrong, because the discussion Dan was having with the front-desk worker had just evolved into an argument. Dan raised his voice loud enough that she could hear his words, even across the room. It got her mother's attention too, and she moved away from the pamphlets to stand next to Tulia.

"What do you mean, we're blacklisted? It's not the tour company's fault a man stumbled into the road. Am I supposed to keep all of them on leashes? This is my livelihood. You can't just drop us out of the blue like this."

Tulia exchanged a glance with her mother.

"I'm sorry, sir, but that is the management's decision, not mine. If you have a complaint, I will leave a note for my boss so she can handle it when she gets in."

"Please do," Dan snapped. "I don't know what I'm going to do if your boss is serious about dropping the tour company. You're going to cut my income in half."

"I'm writing the note now, see? My boss will receive your complaint and be in contact. There's nothing I can do until she gets here. I need to focus on my other guests now."

It was obvious to Tulia that the front-desk worker was trying to politely get him to leave. Dan grumbled but turned and started walking away. His eyes landed on Tulia and her mother, and his gaze narrowed on Tulia's mother. He changed directions to walk toward them instead of the hotel doors.

"This is your fault for telling the police someone pushed that man," he hissed when he was close enough. "I don't understand why you would say something like that. Nothing happened. It was an accident, pure and simple."

"I'm so sorry for the trouble it caused you," Tulia's mother said. "I promise you, I was just telling them what I saw. I didn't mean for it to affect your livelihood. Are you going to be okay? If you need me to call in and leave a good review, I will. Would that help?"

Her mother's earnest kindness seemed to take the wind out of his sails. His shoulders slumped.

"Thanks, but I don't think that will help. The company I work for isn't the problem. It's this hotel. They were partnered with my company, and I had a contract to work out of this hotel exclusively. If they're dropping us, I'm going to have to take up a swing position and cover for the other drivers when they're out, but it won't be the same steady work I have now. I just… I don't know what to do."

"I'm sure once things settle down, the hotel's manager will see that this wasn't anything you could have prevented. You don't control the actions of other people. Whatever happened to Alex wasn't your fault."

"Are you trying to say my family had something to do with this?"

The booming voice made all three of them jump.

Tulia turned to see Victor standing just behind them, likely having come from the direction of the elevator. He smelled like alcohol and seemed a little unsteady as he walked toward them. "First, you say someone pushed my nephew, and now you're saying you don't think the tour guide did it. That means you think it was one of us. Tell me, do you think I pushed my own nephew in front of a bus? Or do you think it was his own brother? Maybe I could see your point if you thought it was Robin, but while she might be a spoiled brat, I don't think she's a killer."

"I didn't mean it like that," Tulia's mother said, taking a step back. Tulia stepped closer to her, keeping an eye on Victor. He seemed unstable.

"Then how did you mean it? Because it sounds a lot like you're saying my family had something to do with this. If it wasn't this tour guide, who my nephew was harassing moments before his death, then who did it? Tell me." He stepped closer and reached out to grab her mother's shoulder. Tulia moved to deflect his hand, but Dan was faster and shoved Victor back. Victor turned on Dan, swinging a clumsy fist at his face. Dan jerked back, just barely dodging it. The front-desk worker shouted as Victor advanced on Dan, his face turning red with anger.

"This is all your fault," Victor said. "If anyone pushed my nephew, it was you."

Tulia heard another shout and turned to see a pair of security guards rushing their way. One grabbed Victor and pulled him away from Dan, and another grabbed Dan by the shoulder.

"Steady, now. What's going on here?"

"This man just tried to punch me," Dan spat.

"He killed my nephew," Victor said, struggling. The security guards exchanged a look.

"Let's get this straightened out. Both of you, come with us." They ushered the men away, ignoring the handful of guests that were watching.

"Let's go upstairs," Tulia murmured to her mother, who looked shocked. "Security will figure this out."

CHAPTER SEVEN

"Let's go out somewhere," Tulia's mother said. They had only been back at the hotel room for a matter of minutes, but the older woman was restless, pacing around the room and making both Tulia and Cicero anxious.

"All right." Tulia glanced at her bird. "Let's go for a walk. We can go to a park and take Cicero. It will be good for him to get some fresh air."

"That sounds nice," her mother said. "I'm going to go freshen up. You get his harness on him."

Tulia did as her mother told her, earning a bite to her thumb for the honor of pulling Cicero's wings through the harness straps. "Don't look so proud of yourself," she muttered. "I'm doing this so you can go outside and enjoy the nice day, you know. You like the results. You should at least tolerate the process."

She fell silent when she heard the sound of raised voices in the hall. She glanced toward the bathroom, but she could hear water running and knew her mother was still busy, so she pulled the door open enough that she could peek out. She poked her head out into the hall to see Robin and RJ standing in front of their room, with a couple that must be RJ's parents, given their looks and ages.

"…believe you'd rather stay here than stay with your own family at a time like this," the man was saying.

"I can't stay with Mom when she's being like this," RJ insisted, gesturing at his mother, who was crying quietly into her hands. "Staying at the hotel was our original plan. Your apartment isn't big enough for all of us."

"That was before your brother died," his father snapped. "You and Robin are coming back with us, and that's final."

"What about Uncle Victor?" RJ asked.

"Victor is an adult man who can do what he wants. He always has."

"And I'm not an adult?" RJ said. "I'm twenty-four. I'm hardly a kid. I can make my own choices, and I've decided Robin and I are staying here. We discussed this and are more comfortable here than staying at your apartment with you."

"It's like you don't even care," RJ's mother cried out. "You don't even care that your own brother is *dead*."

"You were always jealous of him," RJ's father snapped. "Tell me, RJ, *do* you care? Is there some small part of you that actually *cares* that Alex is *dead*?"

"Of course I care," RJ snapped. "But I have to wonder if any of the rest of you would care if the same thing happened to me."

"Don't be ridiculous," his father snarled.

"I'm not. Alex was always the one you cared about. I bet you wish it was me instead."

His mother started crying harder. RJ grabbed Robin by the arm and pulled her into their hotel room, slamming the door shut behind them and leaving the older couple standing outside. Tulia pulled back before they could notice her and shut her own door quietly behind her.

"Talk about family drama," she whispered to Cicero. He bobbed his head up and down, and she smiled. "Sometimes I wonder if you understand everything I say and just pretend not to when it's convenient for you."

"Tulia, dear, what are you doing?" Tulia's mother said as she came out of the bathroom.

"I'll tell you once we're in the car," Tulia said. "We should try to find a park before we leave, since I'll need to route to it on my phone and there isn't any service in the parking garage."

Her mother got a glint in her eye that Tulia knew signified trouble.

"Well, I was thinking, why don't we go back to that park we were at yesterday?"

Tulia blinked. "You mean the one where Alex was killed?"

"Exactly. Since no one seems to believe me, I'm going to do my own investigation. Someone there had to have seen *something*."

"I doubt any of the same people are going to be there," Tulia said. "It's a big city. Half the people there were probably tourists or here on business."

"What about the shopkeepers?" her mother asked. "That café was right across the street. There were other businesses in the area too. One of the employees might have seen something."

"The police would've spoken to them already," she pointed out. She knew she was being hypocritical, but she really didn't want her mother to get involved in something like this.

"Look, Tulia, I need to do this for my own peace of mind. I'm starting to doubt myself. I just… I need to go there. See if anything jogs my memory. What if I *did* see something wrong? I might have caused all this trouble for nothing. How do you think that makes me feel?"

The look in her mother's eyes made Tulia's shoulders slump.

"All right, we'll go back to that park. But I really don't think it will help."

They made their way out of the hotel room and into the now-empty hallway, earning a few curious glances toward Cicero once they reached the lobby. If she had known her mother was going to try to investigate what happened to Alex on her own, she might have taken Samuel up on his offer to come down to DC.

On second thought, that would be a terrible idea. He just might slip and tell her mother all about her own adventures into crime solving.

CHAPTER EIGHT

The park was lovely, or it would have been if Tulia could forget they were there to investigate a murder. Cicero, at least, seemed unaware of the morbid connotations they had with this place. He stretched his wings as they got out of the car, letting out a sharp whistle and then saying, "Come on, let's go," in a copy of her father's voice. She held him up and let him flap his wings and pretend to fly as she walked with her mother down the path toward the duck pond.

"Oh, we should have brought some bread for them," her mother said when she spotted the flock of ducks.

"Bread isn't good for ducks," Tulia said. "I think feeding them frozen peas is what's recommended now."

"Peas, then. Cicero likes peas too."

The bird whistled again, his pale eyes curious as he looked around.

"All right, well, we're here so you can poke around, so go do your poking," Tulia said. "I doubt anyone in the park today was here yesterday. Do you see anyone who looks familiar?"

Her mother frowned, looking around. "No. I suppose we might have to start with the businesses. Hold on—there she is. The macaw lady."

Tulia looked to where her mother was pointing, and to her surprise, she saw the same woman from yesterday strolling down the path with a big blue and yellow bird on her arm. The lady must have been a local who lived nearby and frequented the park with her parrot.

"We *have to* go talk to her," Tulia's mother said. "Come on."

"She probably doesn't want to be bothered," Tulia pointed out, but followed her mother nonetheless. They wove through the paths, finally catching up with the woman as she neared the other side of the duck pond.

"Excuse me," Tulia's mother called out. "Excuse me, you have such a lovely bird."

The lady with the macaw turned around with a

resigned look on her face, but her expression brightened when she saw Cicero.

"Oh, you have a parrot too! Sorry for ignoring you at first, but I'm used to people stopping me and wanting to pet Solar. We walk here almost every day, and it gets old after a while."

The macaw on her arm gave them a sideways look, half raising her big wings. The bird was at least four times the size of Cicero. The African Grey eyed the bigger bird, the feathers on top of his head fluffed up to make him look bigger.

"Sorry to bother you," Tulia said. "We just don't see many other people with pet birds, especially not out and about on harnesses."

"I know, it's a shame, isn't it? Birds are the third most popular pet in America, but I think most of them spend their whole lives in cages." The woman stroked her macaw's head. The bird was wearing a harness much like Cicero's, though larger and made out of a bright-blue leather. "Yours is an African Grey, right? What's his name?"

"This is Cicero," Tulia said, holding him up a little higher. He preened, as if showing off his gray feathers. "Yours is named Solar?"

The woman nodded. "Her bright yellow and blue

feathers made me think of the sun in the summer sky when I first got her. My name is Marian."

"I'm Melissa," Tulia's mother said. "And this is my daughter, Tulia. Would you mind if I took a picture of the two of you together? Tulia has a blog, and she likes to post photos of her travels. This would be a great addition."

"Sure, I'm okay with that," Marion said. "What's your blog called?"

Tulia told her about her blog as they got into position, each with a bird on their hand and smiles on their faces. Her mother took a few photos, beaming.

"Thanks," Tulia said when they were done. "Sorry to bother you. I hope we haven't interrupted your walk too much."

"Not at all. It was great to meet someone else with a parrot."

"Actually, I was wondering if we could ask you one more thing," Tulia's mother said before Marion could leave. "Did you happen to see the bus accident that happened yesterday?"

Marion's face fell. "I did. It was just horrible."

Tulia could practically feel the excitement surging through her mother when she spoke again. "Did you see what happened? Tulia and I were there. I swear, someone pushed that man. No one believes me, though."

"I remember you. You were the lady who was pointing at me, right? I'm surprised no one saw what happened. I looked up when I saw your motion out of the corner of my eye. The rest of your group was all bunched up, talking."

"They said they were looking at you as well," Tulia said. "They all claim they didn't see a thing."

Marion shook her head. "I know at least two people were facing the man who fell in front of the bus. I wasn't looking exactly when it happened, but I glanced up when you pointed at me, then I focused on Solar again for a moment until the bus honked, when I looked up again. There was only a second in between those two glances. I know at least two people were completely turned toward the man who fell. I couldn't tell you who, but I definitely would have noticed if I was being stared at by your entire group."

Tulia and her mother exchanged a look.

"Thanks," Tulia's mother said. "That's more information than we had before. It was nice to meet you, Marion."

"It was nice to meet both of you too. I'll follow your blog, Tulia." She waved and began walking away. "Have a nice day. I hope you get everything about the bus accident figured out."

She walked away while Tulia and her mother meandered back through the park. They found an empty bench on the other side of the pond and sat for a while, Cicero on Tulia's knee, puffing up his feathers at the ducks as they wandered over to look for food.

"What do you think?" Tulia's mother asked after a moment. "Do you believe me now?"

"You're acting like I thought you were lying before, Mom. I told you, I believe that *you* believe that you saw something." She tucked a strand of hair behind her ear. "Either way, if Marion was right when she said the entire group wasn't looking at her, then someone else knows what happened. And if someone else witnessed Alex's fall, I can't imagine why they would lie about it unless there's something to hide. Which means you must have been right. Someone pushed Alex. And there's someone in our tour group who saw what happened."

They stayed at the park a little while longer, enjoying the nice day. It was almost evening when they finally left to return to their hotel. Tulia was tired after spending so much time on her feet, and she suspected she would be walking a lot tomorrow too.

The Washington Monument and the National Mall were in walking distance from the hotel, and they planned to visit tomorrow.

As they walked through the hotel toward the elevator, Tulia spotted RJ, Robin, and Victor coming down the hall toward them. There was a palpable air of annoyance about the group, and a stony silence between them. Tulia and her mother stepped to the side as the trio walked by, but Cicero got their attention when he whistled his alert for strangers approaching.

"Is that a *bird?*" Robin asked, sounding aghast as she came to a stop to stare at Cicero.

Tulia looked at Cicero, not sure how to answer Robin's question without coming across as condescending. She was used to people asking if he was a parrot, or a specific species of parrot, but the answer to whether or not he was a *bird* seemed rather obvious given his wings and his feathers.

"Yes?"

"What's he doing inside?" She sounded disgusted.

"He's a pet," Tulia said, her tone full of irritation. She could tolerate a lot, but she couldn't stand the way Robin was looking at Cicero, as if he was a mangy racoon Tulia had dragged in.

"Weird," Robin said. "Don't birds have diseases?"

"Robin," RJ said, dragging a hand across his face. "Just leave the woman be. Come on, you said you were hungry. Let's go get dinner."

"I don't see why we have to eat at the hotel restaurant," Robin muttered, beginning to walk away with one last glance toward Cicero.

"Well, you didn't want to take my parents up on their offer of getting dinner with them, and none of us feels like driving. Can you just lay off the complaining for the evening, *please*?"

"I kind of wish she was the one who fell in front of the bus," Victor muttered as he walked past them. Tulia and her mother watched them turn down the hall that led to the attached restaurant, exchanging a glance as the trio rounded the corner and vanished from sight.

"I don't think I've ever disliked someone as much as I dislike that woman," her mother said as they continued toward the elevator. "I was thinking of getting room service tonight, but now I kind of want to go to the restaurant just to keep an eye on that trainwreck of a family."

Tulia snorted. "All right, I guess that works. Poor Cicero. Don't listen to that horrible woman, she doesn't know anything about you."

Cicero reached up with his beak to preen her hair.

She stroked his back protectively, wondering just what it was that Robin had against the world. Being unpleasant didn't necessarily mean she was the one who had killed Alex, but it certainly didn't help make her look innocent either.

CHAPTER NINE

The restaurant that was attached to the hotel was nice enough that Tulia wondered if she and her mother should have changed out of the casual clothes they had worn to the museum and the park before they went inside. But there were plenty of other tourists there, and she supposed it didn't matter. A few people were dressed more formally, but a lot of people were wearing jeans and sweatshirts just like she and her mother were.

The Danons were already seated at a table near the center of the room and had their food in front of them. When the hostess greeted them and asked whether they would prefer a table or a booth, Tulia's mother said, "A table would be fine. Could we possibly sit somewhere central?"

If the waitress thought the request was odd, she didn't comment on it. "Of course. Right this way."

They were seated at a table kitty-corner to the Danons. Victor noticed them walk by but didn't do anything other than frown. Tulia tried not to feel like they were doing something wrong by being here. They genuinely did want dinner, and it wasn't like they were going to harass the other family. She didn't know what she would be doing if her mother had never come out to DC to visit her. Samuel gave her a hard time for getting involved with this sort of thing, but most of the time, the trouble found her. She didn't seek it out. Maybe she wouldn't even have suspected foul play if her mother hadn't been there to see Alex's fall.

"This is nice," her mother said as they settled down in their seats. "I haven't eaten out so much in years. I'm going to be spoiled by the time I return home to your father."

"We'll have to ask around and see if there are any other nice restaurants in the area that people recommend," Tulia said. "We might as well live it up while you're here."

Her mother sighed. "I wish I could stay longer. It will be sad to leave for home in a couple of days. I've missed you so much, sweetie."

"I'll be heading back to Michigan soon," she reminded her mother. "I'm going to spend so much time with you and Dad that you'll wish I was still on my trip."

Her mother laughed. "Trust me when I say that's impossible, dear. Where are you planning on going after this?"

"I'm going up to Boston," she said. "That will be my next big stop, at least. Samuel lives in a town just outside of the city, and I'm going to visit with him for a while."

"I really want to meet this man. You talk about him so much; he must be something special."

"He is," Tulia admitted. "We have a connection, and not just because he helped me with Luis. I just wish he lived closer to Michigan."

"You'll figure it out if it's meant to be," her mother said with certainty. Tulia hoped so.

CHAPTER TEN

They continued chatting as they put in their orders, already somewhat familiar with the menu since they had ordered room service twice. They kept an eye on the Danons' table but tried not to be obvious about it. They probably weren't very good at the subterfuge, though, since they both fell silent and looked over when RJ heaved a loud sigh.

"You don't have to stay, Uncle Victor. Robin and I will be fine here on our own. I'm sure Dad wants his brother with him." It had the sound of an argument they'd already had.

Victor snorted. "I doubt that. My brother and I hardly get along better than you and Alex did, we're just more mature about it. Unlike you, our parents didn't let us get away with everything under the sun."

He sighed. "Besides, we've already discussed this. I'm not going anywhere. Not unless you and Robin are going to leave as well."

"Really, RJ and I are fine," Robin said.

"That's what I'm worried about," he said. "You're not fine. You *shouldn't* be fine. I know you and Alex weren't close, RJ, but it doesn't change the fact that he was your *brother*."

"They never got along. I don't see what the big deal is." She sniffed. "Of course it's horrible that he died, but it doesn't really affect *us*."

Victor stared at her for a moment, as if he couldn't believe what he was hearing. Tulia couldn't believe it either. "It does affect him. Alex is *family,* and he died in a horrible accident not even two days ago." He slammed his hand down on the table. "The two of you are acting like sociopaths. Do you have any idea what this is doing to your parents, RJ?"

"At least you're calling it an accident," RJ muttered. He turned to shoot a dark look toward Tulia's mother before facing his uncle again.

"Should I be calling it something else?" Victor asked. "I hate that I even have to ask that. Did you ever think that maybe the reason I'm hanging around the two of you after one of my nephews died is because I don't trust you? I don't want to think that you had something to do with his death, but with the way you're acting, I'm just not sure anymore."

"Are you seriously accusing me?" RJ leaned forward. "For all I know, *you're* the one who pushed him."

Victor shook his head. "I have no reason to want to hurt Alex. Don't be ridiculous." He gave RJ a cruel smile. "He was my favorite nephew, after all."

"Really?" RJ's voice had taken on a new tone, and Tulia wished she could see his face. "Alex and I might not have gotten along, but we did talk on occasion. I think you have at least one reason to want to silence him for good."

Victor scoffed. "Quit changing the subject, RJ. Can you drop this act and take Robin—or leave her here, I cannot stress enough how much I don't care—and go visit your parents? They need you right now."

"You couldn't pay me enough to be around Mom and Dad right now," RJ said.

"And I'm going wherever RJ goes," Robin said. "You're not going to get rid of me. Next summer, I'll officially be a part of the family."

"I haven't forgotten," he replied. "Your gold digging has finally paid off, hasn't it? With Alex out of the picture, RJ will inherit everything."

"Take that back," RJ snapped. "You need to get

over whatever you have against Robin. She's been on my side through everything, unlike the people who call themselves my family. She's got the gumption to do what I don't. She's the furthest thing from a gold digger. I'm tired of putting up with the way everyone treats her."

"We're just treating her how she treats everyone else," Victor said. "No one likes her because she's simply not very likeable."

"That is enough," RJ said, standing up fast enough that his chair screeched against the floor. "I'm tired of you and everyone else bullying my fiancée."

"She doesn't even *pretend* to be polite to any of us," Victor snapped, rising as well. "Why should the rest of us put in effort when she clearly wouldn't care if we all dropped dead?"

"You guys, don't fight," Robin said half-heartedly. She remained seated, picking at her salad as she watched them.

"I don't know, a good smack might knock some sense into you," Victor told RJ.

RJ scoffed. "You wouldn't dare. I'm your nephew."

"Well, maybe my nephew needs punching. I didn't realize just how much of a spoiled brat you were before all of this."

RJ lunged at him, knocking into the table. Food and drink went everywhere, some of it splashing onto Tulia and her mother's table. Robin screamed and pushed away from the table knocking her chair down in her haste to avoid the fight. Victor shoved RJ, and he stumbled into Tulia and her mother's table, grabbing the tablecloth and yanking it as he fell to the floor. Tulia rose quickly, and her mother joined her in backing away. The restaurant turned into chaos around them, and she could see the staff fighting through the crowd of diners to reach them.

"What's going on here?" the first waiter to reach them asked as he took in the scene. RJ was glaring at Victor from the floor. Before either of them could speak, the waiter seemed to come to a decision. "You're all going to need to leave. This is unacceptable."

His statement seemed to include Tulia and her mother. "We haven't even gotten our food yet," Tulia said. "And we weren't involved!"

"Do you know these people?" he asked. "Are you a part of their party?"

"Oh, they know us," RJ said, giving them a dark look as he rose to his feet. "If you're kicking us out, you'd better kick them out too. That old lady started all of this."

Beside her, Tulia's mother huffed. Tulia nudged her. RJ was just being petty, and it didn't seem worth it to argue. If one of these people *had* pushed Alex in front of a bus, antagonizing them even more wouldn't help a thing.

Their silence seemed to settle it. They were all ushered out of the restaurant and into the silent hall between it and the hotel.

"RJ, I'm sorry," Victor muttered, running a hand through his hair. "I shouldn't have let things escalate like that."

"Whatever," RJ said. "Just leave us alone. Robin and I are going to go to our room."

He grabbed his fiancée's hand, and the two of them walked away. Victor turned toward Tulia and her mother.

"I'd like to apologize to the two of you as well. You shouldn't have been blamed for my actions."

"It's all right," Tulia's mother said. "Though I'm a little offended he called me *old."* She sniffed. "I suppose we can count it as a blessing that we weren't kicked out of the hotel completely. It's a shame we never got our food, though."

"We'll find somewhere else to eat," Tulia told her. "I'm sure there are other restaurants nearby."

"Please, let me treat you," he offered. "It's my

fault you got kicked out before you even got your food. I'm ashamed of my actions and want to make up for them."

Tulia opened her mouth to politely turn him down, because eating with a possible *murder suspect* seemed like a bad idea, but before she could speak, her mother said, "We would appreciate that."

"Great." He gave them a weak smile. "I know a place just down the road. We can walk to it."

They started walking toward the lobby. Tulia tried to shoot her mother a look to communicate how bad of an idea this was, but her mother was studiously ignoring her. She realized the other woman must want the chance to talk to him without RJ and Robin around. Tulia could admit that it would be a good chance to learn more about their family, but it still seemed like a bad idea to her.

Victor reached the lobby door first. He held it open for them and followed them through as they exited the building. The only warning Tulia had that something was wrong was the sudden motion of a man-shaped shadow that she saw lunging toward them out of the corner of her eye. Tulia's mother let out a scream, and Tulia spun around, not sure what was going on until she realized the movement she'd seen was Dan lunging at Victor. He collided with the man and slammed him back into the brick exterior of the hotel.

"You wrecked my life!" Dan shouted, getting one punch in to Victor's face before Victor shoved him away. Dan didn't try to hit him again, but he looked on the verge of it. "You got me fired!"

"I thought you had just lost some hours," Tulia's mother said hesitantly. Dan turned to look at her, his face still flushed with anger.

"The hotel reported to my company that I'd been in a fight on hotel property and had to be escorted off the premises. My company let me go. I don't have a job because of you people. A man dying on the tour on my watch was bad enough, but now my reputation is all but ruined. No company that works on the hotel circuit is going to hire me now."

The door to the hotel opened, and a harried-looking security guard came out. "What is going on out here? Do I need to call the police?"

"No," Dan said, beginning to back away. "You know what? I'm glad that man died. He got what he had coming to him. I hope the rest of you do too. You're all horrible people."

"That sounds like a threat," the security guard said. "I'm calling the police."

Dan muttered a curse and took off running. The

guard hesitated. "I don't think I can catch him," he muttered. "But I'm still going to call the police, so they'll at least have a record of what happened in case he comes back."

Tulia nodded. She was all for the police having a record of what Dan had done, because what he said sounded like a threat to her too.

"Did you hear him?" Victor asked. "Maybe he's the one who pushed Alex." He sounded almost hopeful. "Better him than RJ."

"Do you really think his own brother could have killed him?" Tulia asked.

Victor scoffed. "Knowing my family like I do? Nothing would surprise me at this point." He wiped at his bloody nose. "Sorry, ladies, but I'd better go clean up. I'm going to have to leave you on your own."

CHAPTER ELEVEN

Tulia's mother was fuming as they returned to their room after deciding to simply go back inside and get room service rather than finding somewhere else to eat. "I can't believe I defended that tour guide earlier today," she said. "How could he say he's glad someone died?"

"He's angry," Tulia said. "I'm not defending what he did, but we've all gone through a lot these last few days."

"Well, I've been angry plenty of times in my life, and I never said I was glad someone's loved one *died*," her mother snapped. "That's not okay to say, ever."

"I know," Tulia said, a little surprised at how upset her mother was. "Are you all right, Mom?"

"I'm just… I feel so *bad*," her mother groaned, sitting down on the couch. "I can't help but wonder if this whole mess is my fault. I should have thought about the consequences of my words before I told the police what I saw. I wasn't thinking about how it would affect Alex's family or that Dan might lose his job. What if I was wrong, Tulia? What if he really did just trip and fall, and I messed up all of these people's lives for no reason? If I was wrong, I might have driven a family apart and cost a man his livelihood for no reason."

"Well, from what we've seen of their family, they were already at odds. And Dan didn't lose his job because of what you said; he lost his job because he lost his temper."

"I still should have thought about it," her mother said. "I shouldn't have opened my mouth until I thought through the consequences of making an accusation like that."

"I don't think it would have changed anything. Even if you'd known the consequences, you still would have told the police, wouldn't you have? The alternative would be letting a killer get away scot-free."

Her mother sighed. "You're right. I couldn't keep quiet about something so serious."

"Well, if there isn't anything you would have done differently, then the what-ifs don't really matter, do they?"

"I suppose not. Thanks, Tulia. That helps a little. I still feel terrible. I wonder…" Her eyes lit up. "Could you ask Samuel for his help on this case?"

Tulia shook her head. "He has his own cases to work on, Mom. He's not even in the same state as us, and even if he was, I don't know what he could do to help. He couldn't do anything more than the police are doing or that we have already done. I suppose he could talk to the Danons, but there's no guarantee they would even give him the time of day."

Her mother sighed. "I've never been so stressed in my life." Her stomach rumbled, and she gave a dry chuckle. "I guess that doesn't stop me from being hungry, though. Do you want to put our orders in?"

"Sure," Tulia said, accepting the change of subject for what it was. "Let's do that, and while we wait for the food, we can plan out what we're going to do tomorrow. I think we should walk over to the National Mall, since it's so close by. Then, in the afternoon, maybe we could go shopping."

They managed to distance themselves from the mystery of Alex's death for a while as they waited for their food. They made their plans for the next couple of days. Thursday was supposed to be warm and sunny, so they decided to go to the zoo that day. Tulia wished that her mother's trip hadn't turned so grim. Despite everything, she was glad for the surprise visit.

Once their food arrived, they settled down on the couch while Cicero paced across the top of his cage, keeping one eye on their food on the off chance they had something bird safe they decided to share with him. Tulia thought her mother was content to drop the subject of Alex's death for the evening, but she was wrong. Her mother spoke up after only a few bites.

"If you had to guess right now, who do you think pushed him?" she asked.

"Who pushed Alex?" Tulia asked, pulling her attention away from the show they had put on.

"Yes. I keep going over it in my mind. I know I shouldn't, and I should let it go, but I can't stop wondering about it. At first, I didn't think it could be Dan, because he seemed like a nice, normal guy. But after seeing him get increasingly more unstable, it makes me wonder. Maybe he snapped when Alex kept trying to pressure him into taking Robin back to the hotel. He's shown that he can be violent."

"True," Tulia mused. "I'm not going to dismiss him as a suspect, but I just can't get over how Robin and RJ are acting. How could RJ not care his own brother is dead? Neither of them seem to care in the slightest, and that's just crazy to me. *We* care more than they do, and we didn't even know Alex."

"Well, they *were* here to celebrate Alex's promotion in his father's company. RJ seems to believe that his brother was the favorite child, and his brother's promotion probably didn't help with that. He definitely has a motive."

"And remember what Marion said?" Tulia asked, turning toward her mother. "More than one person was turned toward Alex when he fell. That means—if someone really did push him—then someone else is covering for whoever did it. I don't think any of them would have a reason to keep quiet if Dan is the one who did it."

"You're right. I forgot about that." Her mother's eyes glinted. "It must have been RJ or Robin. They seem like the only two who would keep quiet about the other one committing murder. Victor doesn't seem to have a motive, and he seems too suspicious of RJ to be guilty of killing Alex himself."

"I just wish we had more than suppositions," Tulia said with a sigh. "Guesswork isn't going to put anyone behind bars. Which is a good thing overall, since I wouldn't want a legal system where finger-pointing was enough to get someone convicted, but it sure is frustrating right now."

Their conversation petered off, and they returned their attention to their food and the show. Their plates were empty, and the show was almost over, when Tulia's mother grabbed the remote and paused it. Tulia looked over at her in confusion.

"Do you hear that?"

Tulia realized voices she had thought were coming from the television were actually coming from the hall. Raised voices, the sound of an argument.

"I do," she said. They exchanged a look. While there were plenty of other guests on the floor, Tulia's gut told her it had to be the Danons. Everyone else on the floor had been as quiet as mice, and they both knew the issues in the Danon family ran deep.

"Maybe we should go see what's going on," her mother said. "Innocent of murder or not, Victor seems a little too prone to violence. They might need us to call security if things get out of hand."

"You're right, someone could get hurt," Tulia said. "We'll just peek out and see what's happening."

If Victor was willing to resort to violence in a

public place like the restaurant, there was no telling what he might do in the relative privacy of the hallway. Just in case something did happen, Tulia put Cicero away in his cage.

"We'll let you out as soon as everything has calmed down, buddy," she said. "For now, you just hang out in there." The last thing they needed was for him to panic and fly out the door if a fight broke out.

With the bird safely in his cage, she and her mother crept over to the door. Her mother opened it, and both of them poked their heads out into the hall. Sure enough, all three of the remaining Danons were gathered in the hall. Victor had RJ pinned against the wall and was shouting into his face.

"I know you did it. Quit lying to me!"

"I'm not lying!" RJ insisted. He sounded frightened. "I didn't push him. I didn't hurt Alex."

"I *know* you did," Victor said. He took a deep breath. "I saw your brother go off the curb. He shouted *before* he fell. I didn't want to believe it, and maybe I wouldn't have thought twice about it if that woman hadn't said something, but I can't deny what my gut is telling me anymore. You need to stop lying, RJ. You need to come clean."

"You need to stop trying to pin this on me," RJ

snapped. "If anyone pushed him, it's you. He told me all about the affair you had with my mom. He told me that he was blackmailing you. *You* pushed him, and you did it to shut him up so he wouldn't tell Dad about the affair."

CHAPTER TWELVE

Tulia's mother gasped loudly enough that Victor's head snapped toward them. His already livid face went even more red when he saw both of them watching the scene unfold. RJ took advantage of the distraction to push him away.

"Get off me and leave me alone before I call the police. Just *leave*, Uncle Victor. Or I'm going to tell Dad everything. How do you think he's going to react to learning how his own brother betrayed him on top of losing his favorite son?"

"You don't know what you're talking about," Victor said, snapping his attention back to his nephew. "What happened between me and your mother was wrong, and it's over now, but that has nothing to do with what happened to Alex."

"I think it has *everything* to do with it," RJ said, sounding more confident now. "You killed my brother, and you're trying desperately to pin it on someone else."

Tulia felt her mother's elbow bump her arm, and she looked down to see that the woman was sliding her phone out of her pocket. "Just in case," she whispered. "This doesn't seem like it's going to end well."

"It wasn't me, RJ," Victor said, his voice growing tired. He dragged a hand through his hair. "Give it up. I didn't do it, and you're hardly going to convince *me* of my own guilt when I know I'm innocent."

"You don't have any proof that you *didn't* do it," RJ snapped as he lifted his own phone. "I think the police need to hear about this."

Victor snatched the phone out of RJ's hand. "No, you're not calling anyone. You're not fooling anyone either, RJ. Quit trying to pin this on me. I *know* you did it. You're the one who benefits the most from his death. You know your father isn't going to disown you unless the truth comes out, which means his company would be yours one day. And before you jump back into accusing me, you should know that your father already knows about the affair between me and your mother. Why do you think I barely even talk to my own brother anymore? Why do you think I stopped coming over on holidays? We kept the peace publicly for the sake of the family, but that's it. Your information is old, RJ. If you're really trying to pin this on me, you're going to have to come up with something better than that. Now, convince me of *your* innocence, or I'm going to tell your father my theory. What do you think he's going to do if he starts wondering about the truth of it, even with no proof? I don't think your inheritance would be waiting for you anymore."

"You wouldn't," RJ gasped, going pale. Beside him, Robin tightened her grip on his hand. "You don't have any evidence."

"Your father isn't going to need any evidence, and you know it. The police might, but the thought alone will be enough to drive an irreversible wedge between the two of you. I was hoping you would say or do something to prove your innocence, but I can see now it's never going to happen." Victor took out his own phone and started to dial a number.

RJ shook his head. "No! No, it wasn't me."

"What do you think?" Victor asked, turning toward Tulia and her mother suddenly.

"What do you mean?" Tulia asked, stepping more fully out into the hall. They'd already been discovered; there was no point in pretending they hadn't been listening.

"You're the one who said you saw something," Victor said, nodding at her mother. "What about my nephew? Could he have done it?"

"I didn't see who it was," Tulia's mother said. "I don't know any more than you do. I'm so sorry. I never should've said anything at all."

"You don't know anything?" Victor asked, sounding almost desperate. "I need to know I'm doing the right thing."

"More than one person was facing Alex when he fell," Tulia cut in. "There was another witness." She didn't want to say who in case Marion didn't want to be involved in this. "She saw our group right before the bus accident and only glanced away for a second before she heard Alex shout and the bus sounded its horn. That means whoever killed him had a witness, and that witness is covering for them."

"You said your fiancée always supported you," Tulia's mother said to RJ, who blinked at the sudden change of subject. Robin shot her a nasty look. "You said she was the one who had the gumption to do what you didn't. What did you mean by that?"

Tulia realized what her mother was getting at and felt her eyes widen.

RJ looked uncertain. "I—just that she was always pushing me to be better and finding opportunities for me." He wrapped an arm around Robin's waist. "I wouldn't be where I am today without her."

Victor frowned. He seemed to have made the same connection Tulia had. "If there are any two people who would cover for each other, it's the two of you," he said. "I should have known your attitude wasn't the only thing that was rotten about you, Robin. You're the one who pushed my nephew, aren't you?"

Robin gasped, but the action seemed affected to Tulia. The woman's eyes darted between their faces. "You can't seriously believe that. Do I look like a killer?"

"You certainly have the personality of one," Tulia's mother muttered.

"What's that supposed to mean?" Robin snapped.

"You're possibly one of the most unpleasant people I've ever met," Tulia's mother said. "Now, I normally wouldn't say such a thing out loud, but you have done nothing but make everyone miserable every single time I see you. I'm not saying that makes you guilty, but if you're asking us to judge you by your personality, you should know that you're going to come up wanting."

"You do have a temper," Victor said. "But you're right, that doesn't make you a killer."

Tulia glanced at him, wondering if he wasn't as sure that Robin was the culprit as he had seemed a minute ago.

"I'm going to call your father," Victor continued, speaking to RJ again. "If Robin really is innocent, then it was you. You're going to lose everything. At this point, I don't care very much whether you're innocent or guilty. The way you've been acting is abominable, and I'm going to make sure you don't get rewarded for it. Unless you can convince me otherwise, that is."

"No, don't!" RJ said as Victor's finger hovered over his phone's screen. "It wasn't me." He took a deep breath, then all at once, he said, "You're right, it was Robin. She pushed him in front of the bus. She killed him, and she did it on purpose."

"RJ!" Robin screamed. "How could you do this to me? I thought we were in this together!"

RJ pushed away from her, sending her stumbling back. "She knew that as long as Alex was around, I would never get what I deserved. On top of that, he was relentlessly rude to her and talked down to her. She just snapped. I saw the expression on her face a moment before she pushed him. I couldn't do anything about it. It happened too quickly, I swear."

"You said you would keep your mouth shut. You liar!" She began to hit him on the chest. RJ pushed her away again.

"I'm not going to prison for you, Robin. I'm not losing my inheritance for you. It's over between us. Sorry."

Robin gave a scream of pure rage and started hitting him harder. Victor stepped forward to pull her back, and Tulia hurried to help him. Robin might be petite, but her anger gave her surprising strength as she struggled.

"You were supposed to protect me. I did it for you! I got him out of the way for you. I thought you loved me. How could you do this to me?"

"I'm not going to jail for you," he repeated, backing away. "Sorry, babe."

She screeched again, and Tulia had to tighten her hold on her arm before she managed to escape.

"Call the front desk and ask for security!" she shouted at her mother. "Call the police afterward. Security will get here faster."

Her mother nodded and started dialing a number into her phone. Tulia had to focus on pulling Robin back. Victor looked disgusted as he stared at his nephew over Robin's shoulder, and RJ was gazing at his fiancée with an expression of regret. Tulia wondered if he ever would have told someone what happened if Victor hadn't forced it out of him, or if he would have lived his life merrily, reaping the rewards of Robin's actions without any of the consequences.

He might not have killed his brother directly, but as far as she was concerned, covering it up was almost as bad.

EPILOGUE

"I can't believe this is goodbye."

"It's only goodbye for now," Tulia promised. She gave her mother a tight hug, glad beyond words for the week they'd just had. It had definitely been a *good* surprise. "I missed you so much. I miss Dad, too. Give him my love, okay?"

"Of course. We'll see you soon, right?"

"Yes. Just another month or two, then I'll be home." At least for a while, she added mentally, but she didn't want to remind her mother that she might not stay in Michigan.

An announcement came over the airport's intercom that they were beginning boarding for her mother's flight. "I've got to go. I'll call you when I land," she promised. Tulia nodded, blinking back unexpected tears as her mother disappeared into the crowd.

It might not have been the most relaxing vacation, but she was glad her mother had been with her every step of the way. They had helped solve a murder, and in between, they had seen all of the major spots of their nation's capital. Tulia knew she would cherish the good memories forever.

Sighing, and feeling a little lonelier than she usually did, she made her way out of the airport to her car. A part of her was anxious to leave the city which would mean she was one step closer to seeing Samuel again. It was crazy how much she missed someone she'd only known for a few months. But her room was booked for another two days, and she didn't intend to leave early. She wanted to keep exploring the city while she had the chance … and besides, she and Cicero had plans for lunch.

Marion had found her blog and, the evening before, had reached out to see if she was still in town. The inquiry came with an offer to meet for lunch with the birds. Tulia was more than happy to agree. She would love to have a friend who was a fellow parrot owner. Cicero was such a big part of her life, and it was rare to find someone who understood what that was like.

Of course, it would be a little bittersweet to know she was going to leave this friend behind the same way she had left behind all the other wonderful people she had met on her trip. One day, she might retrace her steps and visit all of them again. She wouldn't forget any of them, and thanks to her blog and the wonders of the Internet, she didn't have to. They could remain in contact, even if face-to-face visits were few and far between.

This last week had been a good reminder for her to cherish the people she had in her life. Not everyone was lucky enough to have a good family and friends they could trust. Tulia's wealth wasn't just in her lottery winnings, but in her relationships with her friends and family, and she intended to remember how important it was to treasure those relationships.

Made in the USA
Monee, IL
30 July 2023